W9-ARV-936

N

Distance in miles

0 10 20 30 40

ATLANTIC OCEAN

VERMONT

NEW HAMPSHIRE

MASSACHUSETTS

CONNECTICUT

RHODE ISLAND

Middlebury

Barre

Connecticut

Rutland

White River Junction

Lebanon

Franklin

Green Mountain National Forest

Bennington

Brattleboro

Pittsfield

Northampton

Springfield

Hartford

Waterbury

New Haven

Danbury

New London

Mystic

Auburn

Lewiston

Boothbay Harbor

Brunswick

Portland

Casco Bay

Sebago Lake

Kennebunk

Sanford

Wells

Dover

Portsmouth

Kittery

Concord

Manchester

Lake Winnipesaukee

Laconia

Keene

National Forest

Nashua

Lowell

Quabbin Res.

Worcester

Cambridge

Boston

Salem

Massachusetts Bay

Provincetown

Cape Cod

Cape Cod Bay

Plymouth

Brockton

Providence

New Bedford

Newport

Block I.

Nantucket Sound

Martha's Vineyard

Nantucket I.

Long Island Sound

1

95

95

93

89

91

91

90

91

84

84

95

395

195

495

495

90

93

2

3

6

95

CAROL M. HIGHSMITH AND TED LANDPHAIR

NEW ENGLAND

A PHOTOGRAPHIC TOUR

CRESCENT BOOKS

NEW YORK

PAGE 1: Covered bridges were part of the fabric of early New England. They were covered to keep wooden flooring from rotting. Some were toll bridges. Some of the master bridge-builders moved on to the Carolinas and the Midwest and continued to prosper. Many of the bridges bore subtle flourishes distinctive to the artisans who built them, including windows or lattice ventilators to let a wisp of light into their long, dark expanses. The long ones, especially, were braced by an ingenious combination of vertical, diagonal, and arched timbers sturdy enough to hold heavily laden farm wagons.

PAGES 2–3: The picturesque little town of Barnet, Vermont, with its requisite steepled white church, prompts a stop along Interstate 91 for a quintessential fall New England photograph.

This 1997 edition is published by Crescent Books®,
a division of Random House Value Publishing, Inc.,
201 East 50th Street, New York, N.Y. 10022.

Crescent Books® and design are registered
trademarks of Random House Value Publishing, Inc.

Random House
New York • Toronto • London • Sydney • Auckland
http://www.randomhouse.com/

Printed and bound in China

Library of Congress Cataloging-in-Publication Data
Highsmith, Carol M., 1946–
New England / Carol M. Highsmith
and Ted Landphair.
p.   cm. — (A photographic tour)
ISBN 0-517-18333-1 (hc: alk. paper)
1. New England—Tours. 2. New England—
Pictorial works.
I. Landphair, Ted, 1942–   . II. Title. III. Series.
F2.3.H525 1997   96–43087
917.404´43—dc20   CIP

8 7 6 5 4 3 2

Project Editor: Donna Lee Lurker
Designed by Robert L. Wiser, Archetype Press, Inc.,
Washington, D.C.

All photographs by Carol M. Highsmith unless
otherwise credited: map by XNR Productions,
page 5; painting by Norman Rockwell (from the
permanent collection of the Norman Rockwell
Museum at Stockbridge), page 6; Society for the
Preservation of New England Antiquities, pages
8, 12; Gene Pelham (courtesty of the Norman
Rockwell Museum at Stockbridge), page 9; Brick
Store Museum, Kennebunkport, Maine, page 10;
Lowell Museum, page 11; Newport Historical
Society, page 13; Mount Washington Hotel, page 14;
Stanley Museum, Kingfield, Maine, page 15;
Vermont Historical Society, page 16; Dick Hamilton
Collection (courtesy of White Mountains
Association), page 17; Preservation Society of
Newport County, page 18–19; Collection of
Hancock Shaker Village, Pittsfield, Massachusetts,
page 20; Mount Washington Cog Railway,
Bretton Woods, New Hampshire, page 21

THE AUTHORS GRATEFULLY ACKNOWLEDGE
THE SERVICES, ACCOMMODATIONS,
AND SUPPORT PROVIDED BY
HILTON HOTELS CORPORATION
DESTINNATIONS NEW ENGLAND
RESERVATIONS AND ITINERARIES
WEST YARMOUTH, MASSACHUSETTS
BUSINESS EXPRESS AIRLINES
AND
CAPE AIR/NANTUCKET AIRLINES
IN CONNECTION WITH THE COMPLETION
OF THIS BOOK.

THE AUTHORS ALSO WISH TO THANK THE
FOLLOWING FOR THEIR GENEROUS ASSISTANCE
AND HOSPITALITY DURING THEIR VISITS
TO NEW ENGLAND:
The Devonfield Country House, Lee,
Massachusetts (Sally and Ben Schenck,
Innkeepers); Discover New England, Worcester,
Massachusetts (Sarah Mann and Hope Thurlby,
Media Liaisons); Enhance Travel and Marketing,
Newport, Rhode Island (Ginger Hornaday,
Owner); The Greater Boston Convention and
Vistors Bureau (Larry Mehan, Director of Public
Relations); The Lighthouse Inn, New London,
Connecticut; The Lindenwood Inn, Southwest
Harbor, Maine (Jim King, Innkeeper);
The Manor House, Nantucket, Massachusetts
(Michael and Sara O'Reilly, Innkeepers);
The Manor on Golden Pond, Holderness,
New Hampshire (David and Bambi Arnold,
Innkeepers); The Inn at Montpelier, Montpelier,
Vermont (Catherine Fair, Innkeeper); The Mount
Washington Resort (Cathy Bedor, Marketing
Director); Nancy Marshall Communications
(State of Maine Office of Tourism, Augusta,
Maine); The Old Tavern at Grafton, Grafton,
New Hampshire (Tom List, Innkeeper); Patrice
Tanaka & Co., Inc., South Salem, New York
(Maddy Cohen, Management Supervisor); The
Inn at Portland, Portland, Maine; Preservation
Society of Newport County, Newport, Rhode
Island (Monique Panaggio, Public Relations
Director); The Salem Inn, Salem, Massachusetts
(Diane and Dick Pabich, Innkeepers);
Seacoast Council on Tourism, Portsmouth, New
Hampshire (Carlene Casey, Travel Specialist);
The Simsbury Inn, Simsbury, Connecticut
(Jan Losee, Innkeeper); Stonehurst Manor,
North Conway, New Hampshire (Peter Rattay,
Innkeeper); Vermont Office of Travel and Tourism
(Jackie Ennis, Director of International Tourism);
The Whalewalk Inn, Eastham, Massachusetts
(Carolyn and Richard Smith, Innkeepers);
White Mountain Attractions Association, North
Woodstock, New Hampshire (Dick Hamilton,
Susan Logan, Travel Specialists); The Wildflower
Inn, Lyndonville, Vermont (Jim O'Reilly,
Innkeeper); The Woodstock Inn, Woodstock,
Vermont (John Wiggin, Ski Tourism Director)

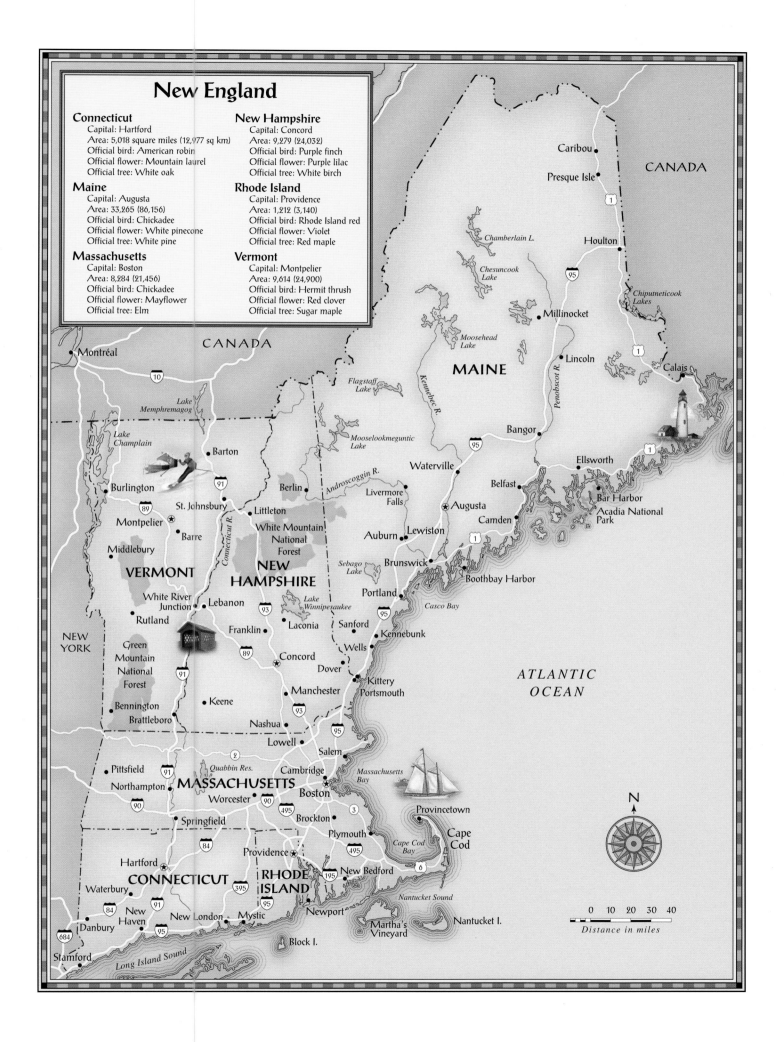

NEW ENGLAND IS AMERICA'S MOST DEFINED REGION. There can be lively debate about what constitutes the West, or the South, or the Midwest. But there is no doubt about the six historic states—Connecticut, Rhode Island, Massachusetts, Maine, New Hampshire, and Vermont—that make up New England. One can live fifty feet across the Vermont line in New York and not be a New Englander, not have the same independent ways or emotional attachment to the past. New England, named by British captain John Smith as he explored the Massachusetts coast in 1614, is a society that was built around the town. Its early European settlers formed small communities, surrounded by a hostile forest and guided by a stern religion that encouraged isolation and a deep respect for privacy. The idealization of New England as a hardscrabble, pastoral haven of feisty individualists is rooted in reality and has been reinforced by the influx of outsiders—"emotional New Englanders" who have brought even more zeal than some of the natives to the fight to retain the region's character.

And what is that character? New England has been called "the conscience of America" because of its history of great orators, emancipationists, and statesmen. But it is a region full of complexities and contrasts. Massachusetts thinks of itself as the place where America started, but Plymouth Colony was founded long after Jamestown, Virginia, and Saint Augustine, Florida. Rhode Island was founded on tolerance, yet its Triangle Trade fed the slave routes. As of 1996, Vermont still had about eight thousand miles of unpaved roads, to barely six thousand paved ones, yet many of the newcomers who are flooding into the state are putting pressure on local road commissioners to bring in the road graders and asphalt trucks. New England's long, snowy winters and gray, muddy springs may cast a pallor over its people, but no other region on earth can match the fire of its fall hillsides. And so go the region's many contradictions.

New England is certainly not homogeneous. Its few big cities harbor some of the nation's most dreadful slums, yet its scenic backroads and small towns come as close as anyplace to being America as it used to be. It is the home of Puritan strictness and the Protestant work ethic, but also Irish and Portuguese and French Canadian *joie de vivre*. It has the same malls, traffic jams, chain restaurants, and gambling casinos as any region. But the real New England—and the states insist there is one just a short distance from the turnpikes and megamalls—is neither fast nor convenient. "Heritage tourists" come to find something that's often lacking at home: genuine, abundant regional history, quirky local color, and an admired plainness of speech, dress, and even architecture has become its own attraction. People drive long distances not just to see maple trees turn crimson or see the site of "the shot heard 'round the world," but also to tour an old mill or hear a Down Easter answer the question "Have you lived here all your life?" with "Not yet."

It is tempting to pin New Englanders' fabled stoicism on their puritanical ancestors; however, there are six hundred thousand more New Englanders of Irish descent than English heritage, not to mention millions of people of French Canadian, Portuguese, Swedish, West Indian, Greek, Italian, Lithuanian, and other extractions who have no trace of Puritan influence. Frugality, too, and eccentricity have been honed into revered character traits. John Gunther captured the feisty flavor when he wrote that New Englanders just "love to be 'agin things.'" Are New Englanders cold and standoffish? The answer is: "None of your business."

Outlanders come looking for the lobster fisherman or the white, steepled Congregational church on the manicured green, images planted in the mind forever by artists like Norman

Norman Rockwell's oil on canvas Outward Bound *(© 1927, the Norman Rockwell Family Trust) was created as a* Ladies' Home Journal *cover. Not showing the faces of his subjects was unusual for Rockwell, but the moody painting emphasizes the loneliness of the sea and the juxtaposition of adventurers and onlookers, youth and age. The painting is part of the collection of the Norman Rockwell Museum at Stockbridge, Massachusetts.*

Rockwell, Nathaniel Courier, and James Merritt Ives. Nowadays, however, three-fourths of all New Englanders live in cities, and there are twelve times more white-collar professionals than farmers and fishermen. The mill communities, the triple-decker tenement houses, the row after row of boardinghouses, and the suburban tracts pouring their workers onto trains for New York are just as much a part of New England.

The region is built around towns, not counties and certainly not regional governments. Maine's sixteen counties, for instance, are little more than judicial districts. It's at the town level that people get together and talk, face to face. March is town meeting month in several New England states. It's a tradition that dates to colonial times. Once a year on meeting day, many citizens gather in town halls and school auditoriums to discuss even minor matters like where new fire hydrants should go.

In Vermont, where the tradition is richest, town meeting day is a Tuesday, and it's a state holiday. Everyone is urged to go; in fact, in the sparse language typical of stern New Englanders, the notice sent to residents reads, WARNING FOR TOWN MEETING. RESIDENTS WHO ARE LEGAL VOTERS ARE HEREBY NOTIFIED AND WARNED TO MEET. Not "invited." Warned!

No such warning is needed, however, to bring out most adults in places like tiny Warren, Vermont, population 500. Warren has no mayor. It is run by what's called a "Select Board," which spends the morning at the town meeting reporting on everything from road repaving to a measure to build a new swimming pool. Even the dogcatcher has a place on the agenda. So open are these meetings that in the printed program, there's a list of townspeople and businesses who are delinquent on their taxes. Party affiliation is never mentioned. In fact, many Vermonters decline to vote in presidential primaries because they would have to declare a party preference.

One oft-heard complaint about town meetings is that people often come uninformed but sound off anyway. There's even a running joke that town meetings are Vermont's "dinner theater." The meal is a luncheon of donated homemade food. A relatively new family knows it has "arrived" when it's asked to bring not a salad or dessert, but a warm dish. As one Warren resident put it, "You may not be a Vermonter—may never be—but you're OK." Such meetings work best in small towns. Bigger communities with more transient populations struggle to keep citizens involved. They're choosing more and more officials via paper-ballot election, so citizens don't have to take a day off work to participate, and moving town meetings to a Saturday so more people can attend.

A common feeling running through townspeople is resentment of the resources diverted to the big cities. In Massachusetts, for instance, fanciful murmurs of another Shays' Rebellion can be heard in the central Connecticut River Valley and western Berkshire Mountains. In 1787, a former Revolutionary War officer, Daniel Shays, led an assault on the federal arsenal at Springfield in an uprising against high taxes and declining farm prices. Back then, the outcry was directed at the new federal government; today, the disaffection is with Boston, which, it is asserted, has drained an unfair proportion of the state's resources. People in central Massachusetts still remember that four towns were literally submerged when the Swift River was dammed to create the Quabbin Reservoir; all of its water goes to Boston. Anti-Boston sentiments are heard over most issues, unless you are talking about which baseball, hockey, basketball, and football team to root for.

When Americans moved west in the mid-1800s, it was the New England village of the Connecticut River Valley that they copied. And when immigration and mills in cities like Springfield and Holyoke and Lawrence began to change the face of New England, some of its citizens worked to consciously promote pastoral images, recruiting writers and artists to spread the word. However, New England was changing, and jobs in the mills helped Massachusetts, the nation's sixth-smallest state, become one of America's most urbanized places. A pattern for rapid growth had been established long before when wealthy Puritan merchants and landowners had founded the Massachusetts Bay Colony at Salem and Boston, just a decade after the landing of the *Mayflower* at Plymouth in 1620. It was in this colony that protests against British taxes and tariffs would prompt boycotts of British goods, outbursts such as the "Boston Tea Party," and the transformation of the Massachusetts Legislature into a "provincial congress" independent of British control. From that point came the inevitable: the outbreak of the Revolutionary War at Lexington and Concord outside Boston, the framing of a Massachusetts constitution that included a bill of rights, and the nurturing of patriot legends Paul Revere, Samuel Adams, and John Hancock. Finally free of British control, the Bay State summed up its tempestuous colonial experience by adopting the motto *Ense Petit Placidam Sub Libertate Quietem:* "By the Sword We Seek Peace, But Peace Only Under Liberty."

Though Boston today is only a modest-sized city, it is by far New England's largest, with a population approaching 600,000. Almost half of Massachusetts's people live in the Boston metropolitan area, but cities like Worcester, Springfield, and Lowell have established their own identities. Lowell, for instance, was once a city of bells. Not church bells, but the bells of six giant mill complexes, starting at

Norman Rockwell captured the essence of New England— especially its main streets and the characters who frequented them— in many paintings.

*That's a young boy,
Charles Lord II
of the Laudholm
model farm family
from Maine, with
an unidentified
woman, c. 1890.*

4:30 A.M. and tolling at intervals throughout the day and evening. To the mills clustered along a one-mile stretch of the Merrimack River went thousands of "Lowell girls"—young women, aged fourteen to thirty, from the rocky farms of New England, happy to get the $3.25-a-week wage, less $1.25 for board. But Lowell, like other mill towns, declined precipitously after World War II, as mill owners succumbed to the allurements of nonunion labor, inexpensive land, ice-free rivers, and tax incentives held out by Tennessee and the Carolinas. In the 1970s Lowell's superintendent of schools, Patrick Morgan, floated the idea of turning Lowell into an "educative city" of industrial museums and heritage trails. The National Park Service subsequently spent $20 million to restore the big Boott Cotton Mill No. 6 as a monument to the Industrial Revolution.

Not just Massachusetts, but all of New England, had built its economy on four traditional pillars: textiles, paper, boots and shoes, and fishing. By 1980, all were in dire straits. Southern states lured away mills and factories, cheap imports undercut the price of New England products, and unemployment and outmigration skyrocketed. And to boot, overfishing devastated the great fleets of Gloucester and other ports—crews from many nations had been simply taking more fish than were being spawned.

Then came the "Massachusetts Miracle." It was a term coined by the Commonwealth's governor, Michael Dukakis, but the boom of the mid-1980s was regionwide. From 1983 to 1987, the median cost of housing in New England doubled as speculation drove up prices. The "miracle" was built on the sudden and simultaneous explosion of the computer industry, high-tech defense expenditures, and financial-service operations. A New England company, Digital Equipment Corporation, developed the "mini-computer," a unit a tenth the size and cost of the old mainframe goliaths that filled an entire room. Soon dozens of companies were making mini-computers and their associated wares. The Cold War sparked investment in secret weapons and guidance systems, many of them top secret but nonetheless profitable to New England companies and states. And the sudden deregulation of banks and other financial institutions produced a rush of "development loans" and wild speculation.

Some economists warned that one or another piece of the "miracle" was vulnerable to collapse, but certainly not all three at once. Yet starting in 1988, the bust hit as fast as the boom. Desktop and personal computers, developed on the West Coast, rendered mini-computers almost instantly obsolete. With the easing of tensions with Eastern Bloc nations, the U.S. Defense Department began closing bases, downsizing its workforce, and cutting the number of outside contracts. And dozens of banks, including the astronomically expanding Bank of New England and the top five banks in New Hampshire, simply collapsed. The subsequent slow recovery of New England's economy—tied largely to tourism, service industries, biotechnology, and health services—has left remaining healthy companies in an envious position. Some are demanding, and getting, lucrative tax breaks under threat of a move to another state.

Colleges and universities bring in millions of dollars from students' tuition and fees, and from their (and their parents') spending in restaurants, bars, book and clothing stores, and laundromats. Tourism is, however, now the No. 1 or No. 2 industry in most New England states. In no other American region are bed-and-breakfast inns more plentiful or in demand, especially during "leaf season." And so popular are restaurants that the region sports an internationally renowned school for chefs and other restaurant workers. At the New England Culinary Institute, based in Vermont, young people pay handsomely for the chance to work at the bottom rung of the food-service business, from chopping greens to scraping bread crumbs off guests' tables, in hopes of someday becoming master chefs. Their laboratories are real-life restaurants, including Butler's in Essex and the Main Street Grill in Montpelier, where students do 90 percent of the work in the kitchens and almost all of the serving in the "front of the house." So fine is the food and enthusiastic the service that many patrons would never know they are exhibits in a culinary classroom were it not for the fact that tipping is not allowed.

New England leads the nation in "environmental tourism." Most visitors to an Atlantic Ocean salt marsh once known as Laudholm Farm, near Wells, Maine, for instance, stow their litter and are careful to keep to the footpath as they peer at wetland bogs, migratory birds, and marsh animals. There is also a farmhouse and big Jamesway milking barn, which were once the centerpieces of a model farm. The entire estate is part of the 1,600-acre Wells National Estuary Sanctuary—Maine's largest stretch of open land. At its dedication, U.S. Senator William Cohen of Maine observed that there is more to the Maine lifestyle than "condominiumizing the coastline."

Guests also get an ecology lesson at the Rose Island Lighthouse in Rhode Island's Lower Narragansett Bay. It was once one of nine hundred light stations—lighthouses maintained fulltime by keepers—that ringed the coastlines of America. Now it is a museum and travelers' hostel with an environmental twist. For 102 years, starting in 1869, the Rose Island light station sent out a steady red beam, not the more familiar rotating white signal. In 1941 the U.S. Coast Guard took over and ran the station until it closed in 1971. During the years of abandonment, vandals stole most of the hardware and the foghorns, tore out all the doors, and even ripped the cast-iron radiators from the floor and threw them through upper windows to the rocks below. But with

The mills of Lowell (left) and Lawrence, Massachusetts, and Manchester, New Hampshire, once hummed, turning waterpower into jobs and profits.

donations of labor and $350,000, volunteers restored the deteriorated clapboard walls, slate roof, windows, and doors. They even installed a weak red beacon—strictly for show. A visit to the island is now an ecological adventure. Electricity use is strictly monitored, showers are short and chilly, and composting and beach cleanup are part of the routine. "It's a mind-altering experience," says the lighthouse foundation's executive director, "without the drugs."

Because of Boston's sway in the New England economy—it's the tourism centerpiece; has the biggest airport, regional newspapers and broadcasting stations; and fields many of the sports teams that New Englanders follow—Massachusetts is the region's pivotal state. It is often seen as New England's liberal anomaly, a by-product of Boston's early Irish political machine, the progressive leanings of immigrant populations in cities like New Bedford, and the unceasing publicity that has followed the Kennedy family. Central and western Massachusetts were never thus, and even Bostonians have been conservative on social issues (remember "banned in Boston"?). Statewide, Roman Catholics are now in the majority, and Massachusetts was the last U.S. state to legalize abortion.

The commonwealth has turned its rich colonial heritage into a tourist explosion. Not just the staple patriots' landmarks like the Bunker Hill Monument and the Old South Meeting House beckon visitors. So do three hundred miles of sandy shore on Cape Cod, delicate shuttered homes on Nantucket and Martha's Vineyard islands, a profusion of great universities, old and beautiful villages along the Mohawk Trail, the homes of literary giants like Henry Wadsworth Longfellow and Louisa May Alcott, and virtually uncountable natural wonders in the Berkshires. There are museums devoted to Currier and Ives prints, shipwrecks, marine paintings, lifesaving equipment, early fire engines, and even transatlantic cable communications.

And in Boston, there's an entire Black Heritage Trail. At the time when the first U.S. Census was counted in 1790, only Massachusetts had declared slavery illegal. A free-black community grew up on the north slope of Beacon Hill, off Boston Common. There, and among supportive whites, sprouted the seeds of the crusade to eradicate slavery throughout the Union. In 1805, twenty-one blacks who had worshiped at Boston's Faneuil Hall formed the First African

The African Meeting House on Boston's Beacon Hill, c. 1885, is the nation's oldest standing African-American church building.

Baptist Church and began construction of the city's first church sanctuary for blacks. Ironically, at the dedication a year later of the brick "African Meeting House," prominent guests, "benevolently disposed to the Africans," filled floor-level pews, while black members were asked to sit in the gallery. The structure, soon known informally as the "Black Faneuil Hall," served as a church, school, meetinghouse, residence, and nexus of the abolitionist crusade. William Lloyd Garrison, Frederick Douglass, Sojourner Truth, and Charles Sumner all declaimed from its pulpit. Restored with help from the National Park Service, the African Meeting House is today the only building on the Black Heritage Trail open to tours.

Connecticut was the second of four original New England states. (Vermont and Maine would be the latecomers to the new United States.) Connecticut was settled, in effect, by squatters who had no legitimate presence on the Connecticut River. They wrote a document called the "Fundamental Orders" in 1639, setting up a government that can be viewed as the oldest autonomous, self-government entity in the world. It is the reason so many Connecticut license plates bear the

The Rose Island Lighthouse was one of 900 light stations—lighthouses with keepers— that once ringed America's coastlines and Great Lakes.

motto "The Constitution State." It was the only British colony granted the authority to elect its own officials; unlike the others, it had no royal governor. After the revolution, Connecticut simply kept its charter, crossing out the name of the king. Because it had no deep-water ports or large cities until the middle of the nineteenth century, this land of "steady habits" had few poor, few rich, and a small mercantile elite. It became known as a bastion of hardworking, ingenious people, skilled at finding industrial solutions to make an honest buck. Then Connecticut, which had little fertile soil away from the Connecticut River Valley, experienced a triple revolution: immigration, industrialization, and urbanization. And in the century that followed, the state led the way in suburbanization outside its own cities and in the looming shadow of New York City to its south and west. In the ultimate New England heresy, many sports fans in southern Connecticut have even switched allegiances from the Boston Red Sox, Bruins, and Celtics— and the New England Patriots—to New York teams. By 1970, most Connecticut residents lived in suburbs rather than in cities or in the countryside, and they had the nation's highest per-capita income to show for it. Though long commutes to New York or Hartford leave little time for civic involvement, Connecticut has a rich tradition of volunteerism in fire departments, local historical societies, and even business offices.

In many ways, Connecticut has long been an American microcosm. The first great Indian War was fought there, against the Pequots in 1636–37. (Opponents of gambling argue that the Pequots wreaked their revenge more than three centuries later by building the world's most successful Indian casino in eastern Connecticut, and that gambling's associated miseries are the ultimate degradation of the Puritan work ethic.) Connecticut had its agricultural frontier, its mill towns, its cities, and its slums. It never latched on to a memorable symbol like the lobsterman or the colonial patriot or a snowcapped mountain as did other New England states.

But Connecticut has become a weekend and day-trippers' paradise, full of quaint inns, fabulous museums, symphony orchestras in six of its cities, top-notch legitimate theaters in New Haven, and plenty of boating opportunities along the Long Island Sound.

Maine, the northeasternmost state in America's upper-right-hand corner at "the end of the line" of continental states, was a part of Massachusetts until 1820. It is almost as large as the other New England states combined but holds only 9 percent of the region's population. Counting hundreds of inlets, its rocky coastline is longer than California's. Houses are few and far between in its dense woods. There are even signs along the Maine Turnpike containing a puzzling series of letters and numbers that stand for the unincorporated and virtually uninhabited tracts of land that can be reached off these exits. Understated humor is legendary in this "Next-to-Last Frontier." For example, summer in Maine is the Fourth of July. That's only a slight exaggeration, for even in August, a swim in its frigid ocean waters, far from the Gulf Stream, feels like sheer folly.

Mainers will tell you they are friendly—at a distance. They are still sizing up people years after they move into the state, and it takes a long time for newcomers to be accepted as "Mainiacs." "Just because your cat has kittens in the oven," goes the explanation, "you wouldn't call them biscuits." Lobstermen still fish the same backbreaking way they always did. Winters are long, cabin fever runs high, and during spring's "mud season," newly thawed dirt roads are all but impassable. Maine is no one's bedroom community, and outside of a few spots like fashionable Bar Harbor, "summer people" have not invaded the state the way they have Vermont, New Hampshire, or western Massachusetts. As if to forestall any more incursions into their way of life, Mainers in the early 1990s voted down a proposal to widen the Maine Turnpike from four to eight lanes, even though 70 percent of them lived within fifteen miles of that road. The state's quiet pride bubbles at the mention of two Maine institutions: the L. L. Bean outdoor clothing and equipment company in Freeport, famous for its conservative but solicitous approach to customer service, and sports at the state university, whose hockey team won a national title and whose baseball team made several College World Series appearances in the 1990s.

The Mount Washington, beneath the Presidential Range, is one of only two surviving grand hotels where wealthy families "summered" in New Hampshire.

For fun in Maine, there are lobster bakes, lighthouse tours, snowmo-biling excursions, and organized moose picture-taking safaris, though the latter are not always necessary to spot the ungainly mammals. In Maine, drivers are advised to watch out first for other automobiles, then for moose—except at night, when one should first keep a wary eye out for the moose, which are darker, taller, and weigh almost as much as a car.

New Hampshire, the only state to border Maine, has had a be-mused tolerance of tourists as far back as 1640, when the first mountain climbers showed up to test Mount Washington. Artists in the "Bretton Woods School" exported the valley's fame, and a joke in New Hampshire is that the state license plate should read not "Live Free or Die" but "Bring Money." The former saying, attributed to Rev-olutionary War general John Stark, was inculcated by William Loeb, editor of the *Manchester Union-Leader*, whose conservative and bel-ligerently nationalist harangues in signed, front-page editorials colored attitudes throughout the central and northern part of the state. Boston's media and sports teams carried more sway to the south. (De-spite his tremendous influence, Loeb, a Vermonter, ironically never became a legal resident of the Granite State.) One county near the Maine border has routinely been the most Republican in the nation in presidential voting, and New Hampshire's cherished tradition as the location of the nation's first presidential primary has led to fireworks and surprises, most often on the Republican side. New Hampshiremen like their "retail politics," and some swear they will not vote for a candidate for president unless they've shaken his hand.

How better to spend a summer afternoon than dropping a line into a Maine fishing hole—then perhaps daring to take a dip?

As evidence of New Hampshire's prized independence and self-sufficiency, the state has stoutly rejected statewide income and sales taxes, preferring to pay for services with some of the highest property taxes in the nation. Stubborn self-reliance is the only explanation most New Hampshire residents can give for their ranking near the top nationally in personal income and at the very bottom in charitable giving.

If Connecticut is an American microcosm, New Hampshire is New England in miniature. Robert Frost once wrote, "It's restful just to think about New Hampshire." It has a modest seashore, spectacular mountains (forty-five over four thousand feet), old country homes, pic-turesque villages, small industries, and even suburbs of Boston. Because its superhighways and most of its rivers run north and south, New Hampshire is a breeze to travel between Boston and Montreal—and can be a nightmare when trying to reach Manchester from the west or Concord, the state capital, from the east. Nevertheless, it is often voted America's most livable state, at least once in the 1990s was named the healthiest, and ranks high on the list of states with surviving covered bridges.

Americans can thank New Hampshire for their national forests. When the gentry of New York, Washington, and Philadelphia, sitting on the veranda of the Mount Washington Hotel and other grand New Hampshire resorts, saw the mountains being stripped of wood they com-plained to Congress. Sinclair Weeks of New York, a New Hampshire native, pushed through an act creating vast forest preserves, in the name of protecting streambanks from dangerous runoffs. The result is that the view of Mount Washington, around which the first national for-est was established, is remarkably free of condominiums, fast-food signs, and ski chalets. Skiing

Sugaring is a spring-time ritual on many New England mountaintops. Maple sap, once hauled in buckets, now often flows downhill in plastic tubes.

is an important industry, however, and skiers and leaf-peepers turn towns like North Conway from sleepy spring villages into full-scale fall, winter—and, increasingly, summer—resorts.

Neighboring Vermont can be differentiated from New Hampshire quite easily on a map: it's the upside-down state. Both states are shaped like ample pork chops, with the "meat" of New Hampshire lying to the south, Vermont's to the north. Once derided as being a "long way from anywhere," Vermont is still statistically America's most rural state. It was first explored from the west and north rather than the traditional route from the east, so it has had a strong French Canadian flavor. For four years, it was even a self-declared free and independent republic, before becoming the first new state added to the original thirteen colonies. For decades, Montreal was the state's natural entrepôt, and it took the coming of railroads from the south to open up trade with the rest of New England. Vermont has also been the region's most liberal state—and among the nation's most patriotic. It banned slavery even before entering the Union in 1791 and sent the highest percentage of its young men to fight in the Civil War. At Gettysburg, Major General John Sedgwick's order read, "Put the Vermonters ahead and keep the column well closed up."

Because "Vermont has what a lot of people want," its rolling dairy farms and climbable Green Mountains have been discovered by developers, tourists, enthusiastic new residents, and parents looking for summer camps for their children. Two statewide planning laws have slowed subdivision and prevented outrageous bespoiling of the verdant state, but many developments have simply hidden themselves in the woods. The outsiders who have come to enjoy Vermont's slow, sensible, human scale have changed Vermont's culture, sometimes outvoting old-timers to raise taxes, spend generously (others say lavishly) on education, and bring amenities like

Chinese restaurants and microbreweries even to small towns. On a less sanguine note, there is a bit of the "I'm here now; close the drawbridge" mentality among new residents of this state that has no big city (Burlington tops out around 40,000).

Just about every time of year is busy on the cattle and dairy farms of New England, but spring is the busiest time of all on Vermont farms. In addition to tending to the usual chores, many farmers trudge up the woodland hillsides, gathering sap to make the state's famous maple syrup. Outside Montpelier, America's smallest state capital, Burr Morse is one old-time Vermont farmer who makes the sticky, sweet liquid, sells it at a little gift shop on the farm, and ships it all over the world. Up on a rise next to his farmhouse stand three thousand sugar-maple trees, the kind that turn vivid red and orange each fall. After a long, cold winter of dormancy, they spring to life, and just before new buds for leaves appear, they produce sap that farmers tap and convert into syrup. Vermont, more than anywhere else on earth, has the perfect combination for making great syrup: a hearty stand of maples, ideal soil conditions, and just the right spring weather—freezing nights followed by warm, sunny days that make the sap flow. Even Vermont's prevailing west winds seem to make a difference.

Rhode Island—"Little Rhody"—is smaller than many metropolitan areas such as greater Los Angeles. It was founded as a refuge for people of different religions who had felt persecuted elsewhere. As a result, not only British dissidents but also Italians, Portuguese, French Huguenots, blacks, and Jews of many nations settled the tiny colony. This helps explain why a statue of *The Independent Man* rests atop the state capitol in Providence. After 1790, when cotton yarn was first spun by waterpower in America, Rhode Island quickly became the young nation's most industrialized state. In the twentieth century it became predominantly ethnic, Catholic, and Democratic.

In the 1926 F. Scott Fitzgerald novel *The Rich Boy,* a character remarks that "the rich are different from you and me." Yes, observed Ernest Hemingway years later, "They have more money." A good place to see what can be *done* with a lot of money is the genteel Rhode Island city of Newport, which boasts one of the greatest concentrations of magnificent homes in the world.

North Conway, New Hampshire, became one of New England's first year-round resorts, with skiing, leaf peeping, and genteel relaxation.

Newport's era as a great seaport ended in 1776 during the Revolutionary War, when British ships blockaded the harbor and turned ships and timber wharves into firewood during the brutally cold winter. Gradually, the city became the nation's first summer resort, as wealthy landowners from the American South, seeking relief from summertime heat, humidity, and disease, built big beautiful wood-frame homes on Newport's bluffs overlooking the Atlantic Ocean. But grand as they were, these houses were mere huts compared with what was to come. In the 1880s and '90s, wealthy industrialists from cities like New York, Boston, and Philadelphia discovered Newport and began building what they called "summer cottages" there. These retreats of the Vanderbilts, Drexels, Astors, and others were much more like European palaces than homes. Each seemed to be more opulent as the families sought to outdo each other. So grand were the gardens that one owner, Dr. Alexander Hamilton Rice, ordered an intricate Persian rug unrolled in front of his gardener and told him to duplicate its pattern in flowers. Most famous of all the summer castles was The Breakers, built in the style of an Italian palace by Cornelius Vanderbilt, grandson of the founder of the giant

New York Central Railroad. His younger brother, William, built a slightly smaller but even more lavish home out of marble, modeled after a garden palace in Versailles. The families sailed together, held debutante balls for each other's daughters, and partied in each other's mansions. But the advent of an income tax, the stock market crash of 1929, and the Great Depression that followed made it difficult for many of the multimillionaires to maintain their "cottages" and staffs in the style to which they had become accustomed. Even some who retained their fortunes simply lost interest, as exotic world destinations opened to them via air travel. Many of the approximately two hundred grand mansions of Bellevue Avenue and Ocean Drive in Newport were converted into apartments. Some were sold to a local Catholic college. But seven of the greatest homes, including The Breakers and the Marble House, ended up in the hands of the Newport County Preservation Society and are open for public tours.

The first Vanderbilt to build a country estate somewhere other than Newport, Hyde Park, or an aerie in North Carolina was Lila Vanderbilt Webb, whose husband ran one of the New York Central Railroad's offshoot corporations. They took the $10 million left to Lila by her father and bought up four thousand acres of ordinary farmland on the Vermont side of Lake Champlain, where they built a model farm, called "Shelburne Farms," in the European tradition. William Webb raised Suffolk sheep, English hackney horses, grain, and apples. Lila Webb created vast English gardens that kept the house in perpetual flowers. The interior became a cornucopia of stuffed hunting trophies, busts of philosophers, and a six-thousand-volume library. After the Webbs' deaths, an heir turned the estate into a demonstration dairy farm and a summer camp for disadvantaged children. Beginning in 1983, Vermont's largest house became an upscale public inn whose profits are turned over to educational endeavors.

Other barons whose pockets were not as deep as the Vanderbilts' sent their families to grand

Newport, Rhode Island, "cottages" were a fashionable summer retreat for these Vanderbilts and other elite New York, Boston, and Philadelphia families.

resort hotels. Little New Hampshire alone had thirty of them. Each had hundreds of rooms, a huge but inconspicuous staff, immense verandas, swimming pools, golf courses, and exercise programs. For entertainment, the aristocracy enjoyed full-dress balls, promenades, and carriage rides to other grand hotels. These pleasure palaces imported fine chefs from New York or Boston and offered separate quarters for maids, chauffeurs, and nannies.

What had turned previously impenetrable New Hampshire into a cornucopia of opulent resorts was a remarkable invention—the world's first cog railroad. It opened in 1869 and ran by meshing its gears with a ratchet all the way up and down the imposing, 6,200-foot Mount Washington—the windiest spot on earth, where winds were once clocked at 232 miles an hour. Once the cog railroad opened, people from all over the world came to see it. Soon, within sixty miles of Mount Washington, fifteen grand hotels opened. Each was like its own small town. It had its own telephone exchange, orchestra, printing press and newspaper, and its own farm to produce meat, milk, and vegetables.

The largest and most lavish of them all was the Mount Washington Hotel, overlooking a long, unspoiled meadow at the foot of the Presidential Range. Today only it and the Balsams Hotel in little Dixville Notch survive among New Hampshire's grand hotels. The Balsams is the site of the nation's first vote and vote count, just past midnight, on primary- and general-election days each presidential election year.

"Living history" museums also abound in New England's historic neighborhoods, mansions, farms, and seaports. At several, including Plimoth Plantation in "America's Hometown," Plymouth, Massachusetts, costumed characters attempt to give visitors a feel for life as it was in an earlier time. One of the biggest "outdoor museums," Old Sturbridge Village, is in the middle of Massachusetts. Visitors can poke their heads inside buildings that had been moved from sites

U.S. Senator George P. Wetmore and chauffeur pause for a photograph in front of Château-sur-Mer, one of the summer palaces along Bellevue Street in Newport.

throughout New England and restored, and watch the tinsmith create spoons, the potter shape dishes, women sew quilts, or the glassblower make a bottle. Old Sturbridge, which marked fifty years of operation in 1996, re-creates life in a New England village in the 1830s, two generations after the Revolutionary War but before the Civil War and the Industrial Revolution. It was a peaceful, pastoral time in small-town America, though young people were beginning to leave for jobs in the new factories and mills in bigger cities.

Portsmouth, New Hampshire, is a delightful old shipping and whaling port that is home to Strawbery Banke, a preserved and re-created colonial village. By the 1950s, Portsmouth's original quadrant had become a wretched slum that the city planned to level. The local historical society and another nonprofit organization saved the neighborhood from demolition, cleaned it up, and turned it into a museum of colonial homes, shops, and gardens. But Strawbery Banke has also ventured into a newer kind of preservation called Twentieth Century Americana. Curators found and began to catalog such items as Ipana toothpaste, Duz soap, Regent cigarettes, "Victory hairpins" from World War II, and an old Mr. Goodbar wrapper from the 1940s. Strawbery Banke also found and displayed kitchen appliances, dishes, an early television set, a washing machine, and one of the first reclining chairs from the 1950s. So visitors can tour the 1736 home of an early Portsmouth potter, then move next door to W. S. Abbott's "Little Corner Store" and see what Portsmouth was like two centuries later.

At Norlands in Livermore, Maine, the astounding contributions of a single family are remembered. Of seven Washburn boys in the 1800s, one became governor of Maine, another U.S. secretary of state, a third a U.S. senator from Minnesota, and the others a congressman, banker, minister to Paraguay, and a naval captain. (Their three sisters' exploits were less well documented.) The Washburn family home and farm have become a center where visitors step into the arduous life of an 1870 Maine family—churning butter, thrashing hay, and even cleaning bedchambers. Among the few nods to modern life: they may keep and use their eyeglasses.

Shaker men and women lived apart and were celibate—but shared worship and chores on farms near Pittsfield, Massachusetts, and throughout New England.

Nautical themes are replete at Mystic Seaport, the nonprofit maritime museum on Connecticut's Mystic River that displays a collection of more than 450 historic watercraft, including

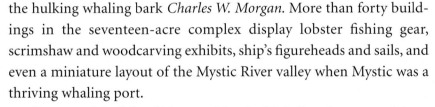

the hulking whaling bark *Charles W. Morgan*. More than forty buildings in the seventeen-acre complex display lobster fishing gear, scrimshaw and woodcarving exhibits, ship's figureheads and sails, and even a miniature layout of the Mystic River valley when Mystic was a thriving whaling port.

For a model of simplicity combined with industriousness, visitors can trek to Hancock Shaker Village in the Berkshires. It dates to the mid-1700s, when a dissident group of religious idealists, calling themselves the "United Society of Believers in Christ's Second Coming," sprang up in England. They were soon ridiculed for their strange, ecstatic forms of worship, which included speaking in tongues, twitching, and trembling. The Shakers fled England for the American wilderness, including an area near what is now Pittsfield, Massachusetts, where they felt they could create a spiritual and moral utopia apart from the temptations of the world. Men and women were equal in authority but slept apart, for the Shakers were celibate. There were no new Shaker babies to help their numbers grow, so they expanded simply by recruiting new believers. By the 1840s, the sect had grown to more than five thousand faithful. But

Mount Washington's amazing cog railway intrigued visitors—including President Ulysses S. Grant—and helped open the rugged White Mountains to tourism.

OVERLEAF: Sheep once grazed on the Boston Common, the point of reference from which the city's historic attractions and office towers are explored. The Common and the adjacent Public Garden are jewels in a string of greenswards, pedestrian malls, fens, and parks called the "Emerald Necklace."

utopia was not for everyone. The lure of free land out West, and the growing pleasures and less backbreaking work in the world outside these humble farms drew many young Shakers away. In the twentieth century, the number of Shakers dwindled to just a few, and in 1959 the only three remaining Shaker "sisters" living on the Hancock farm sold it to local citizens who agreed to restore the historic village so the public could see how the industrious Shakers lived.

Such scenes, far more than the industrial squalor of some of New England's cities, perpetuate the image of tranquil New England. "We aren't Brigadoon, and we're not Disneyland, either," *Yankee* magazine managing editor Tim Clark told the Voice of America in an interview, "although occasionally one worries that we fight so hard to preserve what New England is all about that there's a danger of its becoming a kind of artificial, under-a-glass-jar exhibit." Even *in toto*, New England is a small region—smaller than the single state of Oregon. There are surprisingly few regional organizations (who among the stubbornly independent states would pay for them?), except in esoteric fields like fly fishing and quilting. Idealists plead for concerted promotion of the whole region and greater economic partnership in search of new business, no matter which New England state gets the prize. Instead, each state tells its historic story, extols its undeniable charms, and lays out its own case why it, above all others, offers the most authentic New England experience.

The gleaming dome of Charles Bulfinch's Massachusetts State Capitol (above) in Boston is a landmark visible from many parts of town and across the Charles River in Cambridge. Bulfinch later became architect of the U.S. Capitol in Washington, D.C. The Boston dome was sheathed in copper from Paul Revere's foundry and later, in 1874, gilded. During World War II, the dome was painted gray so it would not reflect moonlight and offer a target to German bombers. Soon after the war the gilding returned. OPPOSITE: Faneuil Hall was Boston's principal marketplace and meetinghouse— the "Cradle of Liberty." It was here in 1772 that Samuel Adams suggested establishing a Committee of Correspondence throughout the colonies to share strategies for dealing with increasingly repressive British rule. Today it is a "festival marketplace" of shops and vendors, but important meetings and speeches still take place here.

Paul Revere's house (left) in Boston's crowded North End is an amazing site, not so much for its architectural qualities and collection of the patriot silversmith's possessions—interesting though they are—but because it managed to hold Revere's huge family. He was twice married and raised eleven children. Not just the crew of the USS Constitution (above) in Charlestown Harbor gets involved in interpreting the history of the heroic ship of the War of 1812. So do costumed guides from the ship's museum. "Old Ironsides" is still a commissioned ship of the line, sailing each Independence Day and on special occasions and firing its cannons in celebration.

Boston's King's Chapel (top right) was a Church of England place of worship for British soldiers. Its builders ran out of money before a steeple could be erected. The African Meeting House (bottom) bears the scars of a devastating fire that nearly destroyed the structure in 1973. The balcony of the building, called "Black Faneuil Hall" because of the rousing abolitionist speeches delivered there, was removed after the fire and later reconstructed during a wholesale renovation. Trinity Church (opposite), Henry Hobson Richardson's Romanesque masterpiece on Copley Square, rests on more than 4,500 pilings driven into Back Bay Boston's soupy soil. The rector at the time the massive church was completed was Phillips Brooks, who composed the Christmas carol "O Little Town of Bethlehem."

I. M. Pei's shimmering John Hancock Tower (opposite) replaced the Custom House Tower as Boston's most recognizable architectural landmark, and its observation deck became a favorite city overlook. From the roof of an older, squatter Hancock Building nearby, observers with binoculars stood watch, looking for windowpanes in the new building that showed signs of shattering. So acute was the problem that each of the 10,344, five-hundred-pound "lights" of glass was eventually replaced. Dunster Hall's tower (left) looms above Harvard University, the nation's first college, in Cambridge. Down the road, at Harvard Square—which is not square at all but triangular—shops, banks, an international newsstand, and a subway station flank the great halls of learning. One, Widener Library, contains the nation's second-largest collection of books.

In one of Boston's "streetcar suburbs," Brookline, stands the birthplace of President John F. Kennedy (right). Four of Joseph and Rose Kennedy's children were born in the modest house before the family moved to larger quarters and expanded further with the birth of John's brothers Robert and Edward. The birthsite is now a National Park Service location offering ranger-guided tours. The Kennedy presidential library overlooks Boston Harbor in South Boston, and there's a statue of the thirty-fifth president (above) on the State House grounds on Beacon Hill. The Kennedy family compound at Hyannis Port on Cape Cod is secluded from visitors.

Sir Henry Kitson's Minute Man statue— a likeness of Captain John Parker— stands on the edge of the Lexington, Massachusetts, green, where seventy-seven citizen-soldiers first encountered the force of seven hundred British troops sent from Boston ("two if by sea") to search out the colonists' suspected cache of arms. Captain Parker's orders— "Stand your ground; don't fire unless fired upon, but if they mean to have war, let it begin here"— are engraved on a boulder near the statue. Eight Minute Men, but no British soldiers, died in the skirmish, after which the British marched to their intended desti- nation a few miles down the road in Concord. The remains of American patriots who fell at Lexington are buried in a modest graveyard on the Lexington green. Lexington citizens often dress as colonists or British troops and officers (above) for visiting groups of schoolchildren.

British forces met their match at the Old North Bridge (above) in Concord. The first Crown soldier fell there to the "shot heard 'round the world," effectively beginning the American Revolution. The event is marked with Daniel Chester French's statue. Dozens more Redcoats died in a frenzied retreat to Boston. In Concord are the homes of Ralph Waldo Emerson and Nathaniel Hawthorne and the exhibit- packed Concord Museum. Concord's Walden Pond (left) is still a pleasant place for contemplation, thanks to concerted efforts by preserva- tionists to keep devel- opers out. The deep "kettle hole" lake— formed by a retreating glacier—along which Henry David Thoreau drew inspiration is now a popular fishing and swimming hole. An authentically furnished replica of Thoreau's cabin stands about half a mile from the pond.

Lowell's Boott Cotton Mill No. 6, now a National Park Service monument to the Industrial Revolution, was a hub of activity for almost a century until it closed, like so many others in New England in the 1950s and '60s. The work on the looms involved threading the machines, checking fibers constantly to be sure they did not twist or break, and changing bobbins and shuttles—and was dangerous and deafening. Boott's bell (opposite) summoned the young "Lowell girls," many of whom worked long hours to send their earnings home to families on hardscrabble farms. From her chaperoned apartment, one girl wrote in 1889 that the weave room's cacophony "could not drown the music of my thoughts."

The 1765 Knowles-Doane House (right) near Eastham on Cape Cod is a classic "half-Cape" cottage, meaning there are two windows to one side of the front door and none on the other. (In a full Cape cottage, there are two windows on each side.) This part of Cape Cod, away from the busy towns close to the Massachusetts mainland, is full of picturesque lanes, artists' cabins—and even wildlife, including coyotes. The Cape also features virtually uninterrupted beaches and a national seashore full of wild and shifting dunes. Offshore on Nantucket Island, cottages take different shapes. Most are clad in uniform gray shingles, in keeping with the island's rigid architectural dictates, but many, like this one (above) in Siasconset, sport colorful flower boxes.

Sunlovers like Kristan Palmer of Sudbury, Massachusetts, appreciate the pristine beaches of Nantucket Island (opposite). Nantucket town itself had turned decrepit as the island's whaling industry declined. Revitalized, it is now home port to some of the fanciest yachts in the Northeast, and downtown became a tourist mecca after it added eclectic shops and epicurean restaurants. And Nantucket retains several lighthouses (right) and other charms. The island's growing concern is the tide of automobiles, carried by ferry from the mainland. OVERLEAF: Old Sturbridge Village is an "outdoor museum" of authentic early-nineteenth-century buildings moved to central Massachusetts. Museum staff in period clothing farm the fields and gardens and lead visitors through chores and demonstrations in the farm fields and more than forty restored buildings.

At Old Sturbridge Village, a reproduction of a nineteenth-century "pleasure wagon" stops at the Salem Towne House (right), which was moved to the restored village from Charlton, Massachusetts. Visitors to the general store (above), get a look at the goods that New England farmers could buy (or get in trade for farm goods). They include a multitude of pharmaceuticals, including mother's favorite—castor oil —cloth and other sewing needs; men's hats (ladies' hats are made by hand by "the widow" down the road); horehound drops and other candies; snuff dipped in molasses; nails and other hardware; but not, as the old-time stores often did, rum.

Like many of the other higher elevations in New England, the Berkshire Mountains (left and above) in Massachusetts burst into glorious color come fall, attracting legions of "leaf peepers." New England's red and sugar maples turn a deeper shade of red and orange than do trees in most other parts of the nation.

The orange and yellow are present all year long but are masked by green chlorophyll until autumn. The red is created by a separate hormone, stirred by the cold nights and warm days of fall. Eventually a heavy rain or stiff wind breaks leaves from branches and sends them swirling to the ground below.

Hancock Shaker Village near Pittsfield, Massachusetts, is a study in simplicity. Light catches a prized Shaker chair (above) in one of the bedrooms, and spills into the kitchen downstairs (right). Pious "Believers in Christ's Second Appearing," or Shakers—so named because of their often spasmodic twitches during religious exhortations—fled ridicule and repression in England and settled on several small farms throughout New England. They were hard workers, raising and putting up food for their own needs in structures such as Hancock Village's 1826 round stone dairy barn (overleaf), and selling seeds and furniture to the outside world to buy additional goods. The celibate Shakers, who believed in the equality but separation of the sexes, all but died out for lack of both heirs and recruits to the sect's strict ways.

A bizarre New England structure is the "gingerbread house" (left) that became the Tyringham Art Gallery in Tyringham, Massachusetts. It was built in the early 1930s as a studio by Sir Henry Kitson, sculptor of Lexington's Minute Man statue. The building's rolling, simulated-thatch roof was designed to represent the hills of the Berkshires in autumn.

Norman Rockwell's last studio (above) was moved across town from its location behind his home to the grounds of the Norman Rockwell Museum in Stockbridge, Massachusetts, which exhibits the world's largest collection of original Rockwell art. There every easel, palette, and brush was replaced exactly as the artist had left it.

A beautiful, stepped birch walk (right) and formal peony garden (above) are highlights at Joseph Hodges Choate's summer home, Naumkeag, on Prospect Hill in Stockbridge, Massachusetts. Choate, a noted New York attorney and U.S. ambassador to England, commissioned Fletcher Steele to landscape an elegant garden that perfectly captured the Gilded Age. Inside the twenty-six-room mansion, designed by Stanford White of Boston's McKim, Mead & White, is a collection of Chinese antique furniture, elegant rugs, and tapestries. The treasures are simpler but no less delightful at the K&J Cooper Antique Center in Sheffield, Massachusetts, and at hundreds of other offbeat antique shops throughout the southern Berkshires.

Flags are fully furled on the whaleship Charles W. Morgan (left), one of more than 450 historic watercraft at Mystic Seaport, a nonprofit maritime museum along the Mystic River in Connecticut. Among the museum and research center's more than two million artifacts are several wooden ships' figure-heads such as that from the Great Admiral *(above).*

OPPOSITE: *The 1896 bronze statue of former university president Theodore Dwight Woolsey sits before the entrance of Dwight Hall— the former college library now used as a volunteer center— on Yale University's Old Campus in New Haven. Char-tered in 1701 as "The Collegiate School," Yale is a cornerstone of the New Haven, Connecticut, economy.*

The marina stays busy at Essex, Connecticut (above), just up the Connecticut River from the Long Island Sound. So does Orion Ford's lobster shack (right) in Noank, Connecticut, on the Mystic River. Twice a day, lobstermen dock at Ford's, which sells the crustaceans to the public at about half the price of a restaurant lobster. OVERLEAF: A tug eases a barge along a serpentine stretch of the beautiful Connecticut River north of Chester, Connecticut. The four-hundred-mile-long Connecticut—the longest river in New England—bisects the state of the same name as well as Massachusetts. Northward, it forms the border between Vermont and New Hampshire. Hartford, Connecticut, and Springfield, Massachusetts, were two cities that grew up along the river. The narrow river valley forms one of Connecticut's few richly fertile areas. Surprisingly so far north, prized shade-grown tobacco thrives there.

A bit of downtown in America's "Insurance City," Hartford, Connecticut, peeks over the trees above the 1899 Corning Fountain (left) in Bushnell Park. John J. Corning of New York commissioned the fountain in memory of his father, a Hartford merchant. Its statues recall the area's original Saukiog Indians, and the hart atop the fountain symbolizes the white settlers of the city from Herefordshire, England. Architect Richard Upjohn of New York horrified Hartford when he topped the new state capitol (opposite) with a Tuscan clock tower rather than the customary dome in 1872. A winged statue called the "Genius of Connecticut" once stood atop the dome, but it was found to be insecurely mounted following a rare hurricane in 1938 and was removed. During World War II, the statue was melted for scrap metal.

The double overhang, brownstone steps, bootscraper, and original front door and hinges of the pre-Revolutionary Huntington Tavern (above), once the finest house and hostel on the Norwich, Connecticut, green, caught Stephen Mack's eye. Mack rescues doomed historic houses, disassembling them after photographing each piece, storing the components at his farm in Ashaway, Rhode Island, then reassembling the structures for clients in other locales. Or, as in the case of Huntington Tavern, he will use a board here, a sconce there, to make another old property whole. "It's like an organ transplant," he says. "Never from a living donor." He took the walls in the north bedchamber (right) down to their 1768 surface, leaving a mottled veneer on the original wood paneling.

In 1846, Henry Chandler Bowen, a prosperous Brooklyn, New York, dry-goods merchant, built a summer home, Roseland Cottage & Ice House (above), in his birthplace of Woodstock in Connecticut's northeast "Quiet Corner." Most of the other fine houses in town were Gothic Revival style, associated with Christian piety. But Bowen, an amateur horticulturist, stunned his neighbors by borrowing a color from his formal parterre boxwood garden and painting Roseland a shocking pink—not once but thirteen different times during the fifty years he summered there. The house did have one sedate, sacred motif: stained-glass windows (opposite) in its parlors. Around Independence Day each year, Bowen threw the ultimate of all nineteenth-century parties for the whole town. It featured speeches, music, and an afternoon of croquet. Four sitting presidents—Ulysses Grant, Rutherford Hayes, Benjamin Harrison, and William McKinley— made the scene.

Rhode Island's white Georgian-marble statehouse (above), one of America's most majestic capitols, overlooks downtown Providence from Constitution Hill. It features the second-largest self-supporting dome in the world. Only that of Saint Peter's Basilica in Rome is larger. RIGHT: The Modern Diner in Pawtucket, Rhode Island, is a "Sterling Streamliner"—"Car No. 4140"—built in 1940 by the Judkins Company of Massachusetts as the latest racy aerodynamic model in its line of "sisters to Streamliners of rail and air." On Thursdays especially—payday in blue-collar Pawtucket—the Modern Diner was the "place to be," but fast-food restaurants put it out of business for six years until Anthony Demou and his brother-in-law rescued, moved, and reopened the diner in 1983.

Rose Island Lighthouse (above) off Newport, Rhode Island, is more properly called a light station, since it had a keeper (and family). Built in 1869, it sent out a steady red beacon until 1971, when the U.S. Coast Guard closed it after guiding lights were installed in a new bay bridge. (Not all lighthouses give off oscillating white beams; Rose Island's steady red was one of a series of signals that gave mariners their bearings.) The lighthouse changed hands several times until the city purchased it in 1985 for $2,300 and turned it over to a nonprofit foundation that renovated it and now operates it as an unusual museum and hostel— unusual because guests participate in an ecological adventure, composting, cleaning the beach, and carefully monitoring their electricity and water use. Some visitors stay in the keeper's old bedroom (right).

New York Central Railroad President William K. Vanderbilt commissioned Richard Morris Hunt to design a Louis XIV–style summer home, Marble House, in Newport, Rhode Island, for his wife, Alva, in the early 1880s. Soon she would divorce him but keep Marble House. Guests were served meals beneath the dining room's gilt relief ceiling (left). Alva's teahouse (above), an example of American Chinoserie architecture on the city Cliff Walk, was a place to contemplate the beauty of nature and "refresh the heart." Mrs. Vanderbilt, an ardent woman's suffragist, dedicated the teahouse at a suffrage conference in 1914. Marble House's dining room (overleaf) was patterned after the Salon of Hercules at Versailles.

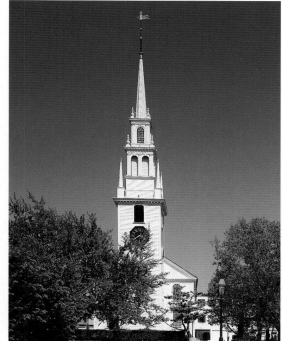

The cherry trees are spectacular in Rovensky Park (left) in Newport. Like some of the city's most magnificent mansions, the parkland was donated to the Newport County Preservation Society. The 1724 Trinity Church (above), modeled after Christopher Wren's churches in England, has a three-tier wineglass pulpit unique in America. Unlike other church buildings in the area that were destroyed during the American Revolution, Trinity was saved out of respect for the Bishop of Canterbury, whose miter is incorporated into the steeple. Since there was no Catholic church in Rhode Island, the Marquis de Lafayette joined George Washington in attending services at this Episcopal church during the war.

Portsmouth, New Hampshire's Strawbery Banke museum (right) features authentic Colonial-era neighborhoods, including these houses along Puddle Lane. Once the city's premier neighborhood, Strawbery Banke deteriorated into a slum before being rescued by nonprofit foundations. Along with their doses of colonialism, visitors are delighted to find twentieth-century Americana displays, including a 1950s kitchen (above). The 1817 Frye's Measure Mill (overleaf) in Wilton, New Hampshire, began as a "carding and fulling" operation, cleansing, disentangling (carding), and thickening (fulling) farmers' wool. Later, it turned out delicate maple and fruitwood boxes as well as simple dippers and other dry measures used when most goods were sold in bulk in bins at general stores.

At their benches at Frye's Measure Mill (above), craftsworkers made and repaired their own molds; bent and shaped thinly peeled, soaked wood into containers called measures (including dippers called "piggins"; and added pegs, brads, and handles. Even today, the work area is unheated. In New Hampshire's bitter wintertime, workers follow the warming sun from room to room and task to task. Today the mill is run by Harley Savage— who had studied oceanography and art but elected to join his father in business— and his wife, Pam. They're still making utilitarian measures and dippers but have added a line of beautiful Shaker and "pantry" boxes. "Restoration here is an everyday event," Savage says. "Our millwright is always crafting new parts in the machine shop or removing and oiling and restitching the big leather drive belts. There's no place to go for spare parts."

World-renowned sculptor Augustus Saint-Gaudens built a studio (right) to replace the hay barn out of which he had been working at his home in rural Cornish, New Hampshire. Saint-Gaudens, an Irish-born, French-trained New Yorker who had gained fame creating heroic statues in several cities—including Chicago during the great Colombian Exposition of 1893—originally bought the site, including a home in a former tavern, as a summer retreat. His Adams Memorial statue (above), considered one of his most important works, is a copy of the figure in Rock Creek Cemetery in Washington, D.C., that was commissioned by historian Henry Adams for his wife's grave.

The Durgin Bridge (left) over the Swift River, near Tamworth, New Hampshire, completes an icescape worthy of Currier and Ives. In North Conway, New Hampshire, Treffle Bolduc (above) became a terrific—but most unlikely—snowshoe maker. He had been trained as a violinist—a classical musician, not a fiddler of the sort that's popular in other French-speaking families—and was concertmaster for the Manchester, New Hampshire, orchestra when he quit and decided to live by his wits in the woods. He learned snowshoe making from Indians in Quebec and now crafts the shoes by hand in a small shop and sells them all over the world.

Sunset glows over the Ammonoosuc River (left) in northern New Hampshire. Such places remind visitors of the still-pastoral nature of most of New England. Strong preservation movements in all six of the region's states have helped protect such sites from rampant development. Even in popular tourist destinations such as these White Mountains, it's possible to hike just a few hundred yards off most paved roads and find similar tranquillity. The irony is that nostalgia for slower times is attracting newcomers who can sometimes spoil the simplicity they came to enjoy. But at places like the Moultonborough Country Store (above) in New Hampshire, both visitors and nostalgia are heartily welcomed. Residents have permitted discount megastores and fast-food restaurants only grudging inroads in rural New England.

The Mount Washington Hotel (right) was once a great resort, attracting guests from all over the world. After lean years in which all but one other New Hampshire grand hotel burned or failed, the Mount Washington is again the "Grande Dame of the White Mountains." The hotel, which hosted the 1944 Bretton Woods International Monetary Conference that led to the establishment of the World Bank, was rescued from the brink of receivership in the early 1990s by four area couples. They steadily refurbished guest rooms, public spaces, the "Cave" basement entertainment area, and the nine-hundred-foot veranda (above). The hotel and associated inns still run the unforgettable Mount Washington Cog Railway (overleaf), the "Little Train That Could" climb the world's second-steepest railway track. Long before there were autos, telephones, or electric lights, these powerful steam trains were ratcheting up the highest peak in the Northeast.

Chopping and laying in plenty of firewood for the winter (right) is a good idea in frigid New Hampshire. More traditional lumbering is still big business—especially in Maine, which has more firs than maples—and sawmills are plentiful throughout the region. But conservationists and environmentalists, concerned about the effects of denuding forests, have succeeded in getting millions of acres of timberland declared off-limits to cultivation. Highland Croft (above) outside Littleton, New Hampshire, was long a working dairy farm but is now rental property. There's also a large lodge up the hill on the grounds. Ever since a dam was erected on the wild Ammonoosuc River in 1790 and a gristmill and sawmill were constructed, Littleton has been the hub of the rugged White Mountains.

The Balsams Hotel (above) in far-northern New Hampshire—note the Canadian as well as American flag—gets the attention of the world every four years when the first votes of the New Hampshire Primary are cast there at midnight and immediately tallied. The grand hotel is located in a town with a colorful name: Dixville Notch, the "Switzerland of the Nation." There are several such notches, or cuts, through the craggy New Hampshire mountains. An old stone portal (opposite) and stone fence (overleaf) are evidence that the Balsams has been in business a long time. It began as the Dix House, a twenty-five-room inn, soon after the Civil War. In 1895 a wealthy Philadelphia inventor, Henry Hale, purchased, renamed, and began to enlarge the hotel. The estate is bigger than Manhattan Island. It offers hiking, mountain biking, fishing, and natural-history programs.

Winter brings special beauty to Vermont's tiny state capital, Montpelier (left), as the capitol dome gleams through the trees, and smoke and mist rise from buildings. Vermont winters inspired poets like Robert Frost. They also mean plenty of activity on mountainsides like Mount Mansfield at Stowe ski resort (above) in the Green Mountains, from which the state gets its name (vert mont). The oldest combination downhill–cross country ski race in the country is held at Stowe each February. Many Vermonters are hardy, outdoors people for whom winter is a time of awakening to outdoor activities, including snowmobiling, snowboarding, snowshoeing, and sleigh rides. They and visitors can even take advantage of an around-the-state cross country skiing adventure that takes them to four country inns along the Catamount Trail.

Among the most picturesque of all Vermont towns is Woodstock, where a long park of evergreens, statues, and gazebos (left) turns into a winter wonderland. Sleigh rides (above) are just one delight at the Billings Farm & Museum, a living museum of Vermont's rural heritage—and a working farm that has raised championship Jersey dairy cows since 1871. The farm's calendar includes plowing matches,

cornhusking, barn dances, and a day when visitors learn about heirloom seeds. OPPOSITE: *Each spring, even when there's still snow on the ground, Montpelier, Vermont, farmer Burr Morse— like thousands of other Vermonters— turns his spread into a maple sugaring operation. Vermont's climate is ideal for making the sweet confection, and Morse ships syrup and maple candy all over the world.*

The public library in Guildhall, Vermont (above), built in 1900, was once a Masonic hall. Guildhall was settled in 1764, ten years after Guildhall Falls was discovered. This remote town in Vermont's "Northern Kingdom" was the frontier during the French and Indian War. One could spend an entire long vacation just visiting and photographing New England steepled churches, like the White Church (opposite), a former Baptist church that is now a community church in Grafton, Vermont. The factors to look for: clean lines, white paint, high steeple, preferably a clear view across a green unobstructed by signs or telephone wires, and unostentatious windows. And there are plenty of small towns for these places of worship that seem to signify New England's humble piety. The state's largest city, Burlington, barely reaches 40,000 population, and Montpelier, at about 8,000, is the nation's smallest capital city.

Unlike her Vanderbilt siblings, Lila Vanderbilt Webb and her husband, William Seward Webb—who ran the Vanderbilts' Wagner Palace Car railroad company—did not turn to Newport, Hyde Park, or the North Carolina mountains to build a country estate. They chose four thousand acres of farmland on Lake Champlain, near the tiny town of Shelburne, Vermont, and built a mansion and model farm. The five-story barn (above) housed a blacksmith shop, workshops, management offices, and stalls for eighty teams of horses. The manor's tea room (right) was used for breakfast and informal dinners. Today Shelburne Farms' Shingle Style manor—imposing by most standards but a mere cottage compared to most Vanderbilt family estates—is a public inn whose profits go to educational endeavors.

Once abandoned and bedraggled, Officers' Row (opposite), straddling the border between Colchester and Essex, Vermont, was rehabilitated into affordable condominiums and loft apartments. The complex, which housed U.S. Cavalry officers at Fort Ethan Allen beginning in 1894, included a spacious parade ground and a gazebo (above) big enough to hold the town band. In order to keep units reasonably priced, much of the restoration was left to the new owners, who were given handbooks and instructions on how to restore woodwork, cabinets, and fir floors. OVERLEAF: The 460-foot, two-span covered bridge between Cornish, New Hampshire, and Windsor, Vermont— built in 1866 for $9,000—is the nation's longest wooden bridge and the longest two-span covered bridge in the world. It was a private toll bridge until 1936 and later, in 1943, was purchased by the State of New Hampshire.

A trip to New England is often a search for simple pleasures: a stop by the pond at Windsor (opposite), the "Birthplace of Vermont"; an autumn array outside the Wildflower Inn bed and breakfast in Lyndonville, Vermont (above); a quiet drive down a beautiful road (overleaf) in the Carrabassett Valley of western Maine. Just as Mark Twain wrote that there is "a sumptuous variety about the New England weather that compels the stranger's admiration— and regret," there is a cornucopia of natural wonders to appreciate. The surroundings, like the leaves, can be understated, then fiery. New England is not America's coldest, wettest, highest, or greenest region, and certainly not the wealthiest, but it's a lot of all these things— and the most historic and idiosyncratic. It's a place where the cliché rings true: the more things change, the more they stay the same.

Maine's rocky coast-
line is dotted with
quaint inlets, includ-
ing Northeast Harbor
(left) and Southwest
Harbor (above),
where fishing and
oyster fleets moor
among pleasure boats.
OVERLEAF: Norlands
in Livermore, Maine,
is a working farm and
living-history center
at which visitors leave
behind the vestiges of
twentieth-century life
and, briefly, step into
the arduous world of a
Maine family of 1870.

At Norlands that
family, the Wash-
burns, was a dynasty.
Consider the seven
sons of Israel and
Patty Washburn:
one became governor
of Maine; another
secretary of state
under Ulysses S.
Grant; a third
a U.S. senator from
Minnesota; and the
others, respectively, a
Maine banker, a U.S.
congressman from
Wisconsin, a minister
to Paraguay, and a
U.S. Navy captain.

Wells Reserve at Laudholm Farm is the ideal destination for an "environmental tourist." At this estuarine research reserve on an Atlantic Ocean salt marsh once known as Laudholm Farm, visitors observe ducks, piping plovers, least terns, moose, mink, river otters, and even bobcats—and get a thorough grounding in the ecology of a wetland meadow by the sea. Part of the sanctuary includes the Rachel Carson National Wildlife Reserve, named for the author of Silent Spring. The giant Jamesway Barn (above and right), built mostly from precut parts provided by the James Company, contained milking pens and room for 120 tons of hay. OVERLEAF: The Carrabassett River, extending from high ski country to the lowlands of western Maine, is a scenic treasure and fisherman's paradise.

Index

Unfortunately, hulking moose don't wait until they see a crossing sign to crash out of the brush and into traffic on Maine roads, especially at dawn and dusk.

Page numbers in italics refer to illustrations.

Adams, Samuel, 9, 24
African Meeting House, 12, *12*, 28
Ammonoosuc River, *93, 98*

Balsams resort, 19, *101*
Barnet, Vermont, *4*
Berkshire Mountains, 9, 12, 20, *49, 55*
Billings Farm & Museum, *107*
Black Heritage Trail, 12
Bolduc, Treffle, *91*
Boott Cotton Mill No. 6, 10, *38*
Boston Common, 21
Boston Tea Party, 9
Bretton Woods artists' school, 15
Bretton Woods International Monetary Conference, *94*
Brooks, Phillips, 28
Bulfinch, Charles, 24

Cape Cod, 12, *32, 40*
Carrabassett River, *124*
Choate, Joseph Hodges, *56*
Clark, Tim, 21
Cohen, William, 11
Concord, Massachusetts, and battle, 9, *35, 37*
Connecticut River and Valley, 9, *12–13, 62*
Connecticut State Capitol, *67*
Corning Fountain, *67*
Courier, Nathaniel and James Merritt Ives, 8
Covered bridges, *4, 91, 112*

Digital Equipment Corporation, 10
Dixville Notch, New Hampshire, *101*
Durgin Bridge, *91*

Emerson, Ralph Waldo, *37*
Essex, Connecticut, marina, *62*

Faneuil Hall, 12, *24*
Fitzgerald, F. Scott, 17
Ford's lobster shack (Noank, Connecticut), *62*
French, Daniel Chester, *37*
Frost, Robert, 15
Frye's Measure Mill, *81, 86*

Grant, Ulysses S., 21, *70*
Green Mountains, *105*
Guildhall, Vermont, Public Library, *108*

Hale, Henry, *101*
Hancock Shaker Village. *See* Shakers
Harvard University, 21
Hancock Tower, *31*
Highland Croft, *98*
Huntington Tavern, *68*

K&J Antique Center (Sheffield, Massachusetts), *56*
Kennedy, John F. and Kennedy family, 11, *32*
King's Chapel, 28
Kitson, Henry, *35, 55*
Knowles-Doane House (Cape Cod, Massachusetts), *40*

Laudholm Farm, *10*, 11, *124*
Leaf "peepers," 11, 16, *49*
Lexington, Massachusetts and battle, 9, *35*
L. L. Bean outdoor store, 14
Loeb, William, 15
Lowell, Massachusetts, 9–10, *11, 38*

Mack, Stephen, *68*
Maine wisdom, 14
Marble House, 18, *77*
Massachusetts Bay Colony, 9
"Massachusetts Miracle," 10
Massachusetts State Capitol, *24*
Minute Man statue, Lexington, Massachusetts, *35, 55*
Modern Diner, *70*
Mohawk Trail, 12
Moose, 14, *128*
Morse, Burr, 17, *107*
Mount Washington Cog Railway, 19, 21, *94*
Mount Washington Hotel & Resort, 15, 19, 21, *94*
Mystic Seaport, 20, *61*

Nantucket, Massachusetts, 12, *40, 42*
Naumkeag, *56*
New England Culinary Institute, 11
Newport, Rhode Island, *18*, 19, *74, 77, 81*
Norlands living-history center, 20, *121*
North Conway, New Hampshire, 17
Northeast Harbor, Maine, *121*

Officers' Row, *112*
Old North Bridge (Concord, Massachusetts), *37*
Old South Meeting House, 12
Old Sturbridge Village, 19–20, *42, 46*

Pei, I. M., *31*
Plimoth Plantation, 19
Plymouth Colony, 7

Revere, Paul, 9, *24, 27*
Rhode Island State Capitol, *72*
Rice, Dr. Alexander Hamilton, 17
Richardson, Henry Hobson, 28
Rockwell Museum at Stockbridge, *7, 55*
Rockwell, Norman, *7, 8, 9, 55*
Rose Island Lighthouse, 11–12, *13, 74*
Roseland Cottage & Ice House, *8, 70*

Saint-Gaudens, Augustus and studio, *88*
Shakers and Hancock Shaker Village, 20–21, *20, 50, 86*
Shays' Rebellion, 9
Shelburne Farms, 18, *110*
Steele, Fletcher, *56*
Stowe, Vermont, ski resort, 18, *105*
Strawbery Banke, 20, *81*
Sugaring, maple, 16, *17, 107*

Thoreau, Henry David, *37*
Town meetings, 8
Trinity Church (Boston), 28
Trinity Church (Newport, Rhode Island), *81*
Twain, Mark, *117*
Tyringham, Massachusetts, "gingerbread house," *55*

Upjohn, Richard, *67*
USS *Constitution*, *27*

Vanderbilt, Cornelius, 17–18
Vanderbilt, William K. and Alva, 18, *77*
Vermont State Capitol, *105*

Walden Pond, *37*
Warren, Vermont, 8
Washburn family, 20, *121*
Webb, William Seward and Lila Vanderbilt, 18, *110*
Weeks, Sinclair, 15
Wells Reserve at Laudholm Farm, 11, *121*
Wetmore, George P., *19*
White Church, The (Grafton, Vermont), *108*
White Mountains, 21, *93, 98*
Wildflower Inn, Lyndonville, Vermont, *117*
Windsor, Vermont, *117*
Woodstock, Connecticut, 8
Woodstock, Vermont, *107*

Yale University, *61*